Learning to Read, Step by Step!

Ready to Read   Preschool–Kindergarten
• big type and easy words • rhyme and rhythm • picture clues
For children who know the alphabet and are eager to begin reading.

Reading with Help   Preschool–Grade 1
• basic vocabulary • short sentences • simple stories
For children who recognize familiar words and sound out new words with help.

Reading on Your Own   Grades 1–3
• engaging characters • easy-to-follow plots • popular topics
For children who are ready to read on their own.

Reading Paragraphs   Grades 2–3
• challenging vocabulary • short paragraphs • exciting stories
For newly independent readers who read simple sentences with confidence.

Ready for Chapters   Grades 2–4
• chapters • longer paragraphs • full-color art
For children who want to take the plunge into chapter books but still like colorful pictures.

STEP INTO READING® is designed to give every child a successful reading experience. The grade levels are only guides; children will progress through the steps at their own speed, developing confidence in their reading. The F&P Text Level on the back cover serves as another tool to help you choose the right book for your child.

Remember, a lifetime love of reading starts with a single step!

Visit us on the Web!
Seussville.com
StepIntoReading.com
pbskids.org/catinthehat
treehousetv.com

Educators and librarians, for a variety of teaching tools, visit us at
RHTeachersLibrarians.com

Library of Congress Cataloging-in-Publication Data
Rabe, Tish.
The tree doctor / by Tish Rabe ; from a script by Bernice Vanderlaan ; illustrated by Tom Brannon.
    p. cm. — (Step into reading. Step 2)
"Based in part on The Cat in the Hat Knows a Lot About That! TV series (Episode 117)."—
Copyright p.
ISBN 978-0-375-86957-0 (trade) — ISBN 978-0-375-96957-7 (lib. bdg.)
ISBN 978-0-375-98149-4 (ebook)
I. Vanderlaan, Bernice. II. Brannon, Tom. III. Cat in the hat knows a lot about that (Television program). IV. Title.
PZ8.3.R1145Tre 2013 [E]—dc23 2011048246

Printed in the United States of America
10 9 8 7 6 5

This book has been officially leveled by using the F&P Text Level Gradient™ Leveling System.

The Tree Doctor

by Tish Rabe

from a script by Bernice Vanderlaan

illustrated by Tom Brannon

Random House 🏠 New York

"Breakfast!" called Sally. "The pancakes are hot! Let's find out how much maple syrup we've got." "Trees give sap to make syrup," said Nick, "but this one is so small, we can't make any syrup. No fun!"

"I smell pancakes!" the Cat cried.
"Oh, I hope I am right.
I love golden pancakes,
all fluffy and light,
with sweet maple syrup.

Oh, pour me some, please!

It's my favorite thing

that we get from the trees."

"We've got pancakes," said Nick.
"But unfortunately,
   no sap to make syrup
   from our maple tree."

"Not to worry!" the Cat said.

"Today I'll take you

to meet the Tree Doctor.

He'll know what to do."

"Meet Dr. Twiggles!

He takes care of trees.

He swings through the branches

and hangs by his knees!"

"Hello," said the doctor.
"Yes, it's up to me
to respond to and treat
every tree-mergency!"

Dr. Twigberry Twiggles
2 Spruce Street
Wild Woolly Wood

If your pine is in pain or your oak's not OK,
call me night or day. I'll be there right away.

11

"Now, what brings you three
to the Wild Woolly Wood?"
"Our tree's not growing,"
answered Nick, "as it should."

"Little tree," said the doctor,

"how are you feeling?

Are your twigs in a twist?

Has your bark started peeling?"

"Hmm . . . color's nice and dark.

Stem is not bumpy.

Branches aren't brittle.

Twigs are not lumpy.

But these leaves are drooping,

and that means, I'd say,

I should check your tree's roots

and do so right away."

"Check the roots?" Sally asked.

"How can you do that?"

"To the Thinga-ma-jigger!"

cried the Cat in the Hat.

"Flip the Thrilla-ma-driller
and we'll see if it's ill.
If you've never seen tree roots,
well, soon we all will!"

"Look at that," said Nick.
"This really is neat.
The roots of a tree
are like a tree's feet."

"AbsoROOTly!" the Cat cried.
"I happen to know
roots soak up food and water
and help a tree grow."

"I've got it!" the doc said.

"Now I see why

your tree isn't growing.

The soil is too dry."

"It needs water?" the Cat asked.

"I know what to do.

This is a job

for Thing One and Thing Two!"

Those two Things jumped out,
and they gave a big yank
to the crank on the side
of the Thinga-ma-tank.

But they turned it too far
and they turned it too fast.
Water shot out in a
soaking-wet blast!

"Good job!" said the doc.
"But our work is not done.
To get healthy, your tree
needs to get lots of sun."
"I know!" cried the Cat.
"Your tree will feel right
when my Brighta-ma-lighter
gives it sunlight."

"Now just wait," said the doc. "In forty years you can tap your tree and make syrup from the maple tree sap."

"Forty years!" said Nick.
"When our tree is that old,
our stack of pancakes
will REALLY be cold!"

"No problem!" said the doc.
"For I have right here
some syrup I made
in the spring of last year.

And I have something else—
a bag of maple keys,
full of maple tree seeds
to grow even more trees."

Back home, Nick said,

"This syrup is good

and I had lots of fun

in the Wild Woolly Wood."

"Eat up!" said the Cat.

"Then I need your help, please.

After breakfast let's go

and plant . . .

". . . more maple trees!"